ACKNOWLEDGEMENTS
Thank you to Sally Campbell for all her help and hard work and to
Lina Nicolli, Peter Robinson and Mary Phillips for their work on the
production. Thanks to Jim Fagan and Fran Manning for their helpful
comments, and to the many others who contributed ideas and
insights. Special thanks to Liam Brown, Ron Singer and Jan Blake for
their encouragement, to Rhys Williams for his love and patience and
to Andy Brown for all his support.

ABOUT THE AUTHOR
Siobhan Brown is a museum worker and activist from east London.
She is on the editorial board of *Socialist Review*.

COVER PHOTOGRAPH: Portrait of Eleanor Marx.
INSIDE FRONT PHOTOGRAPH: A stevedores' float during the 1889 dock
strike, part of a procession assembled in East India Dock Road, London.
INSIDE BACK ILLUSTRATION: The International platform at the 1891
May Day rally in Hyde Park, published in the *Illustrated London News*.
Eleanor Marx stands in the foreground; Edward Aveling is speaking.

Published by Bookmarks Publications 2015
ISBN print edition: 978-1-909026-77-3
ISBN Kindle: 978-1-909026-80-3
ISBN ePub: 978-1-909026-81-0
ISBN PDF: 978-1-909026-82-7
Series designed by Noel Douglas (noel@noeldouglas.net)
Printed by Halstan Printing Group

A Rebel's Guide to
ELEANOR MARX

SIOBHAN BROWN

★ 1: INTRODUCTION

Eleanor Marx was an agitator, an organiser and a writer. She threw herself into struggles against imperialism, racism and sexism. She was surrounded her whole life by activists — and became one of the greatest activists of her time. She was so much more than just the youngest daughter of the great revolutionary Karl Marx.

She was shaped, as we all are, by the times she lived and worked in. From the Paris Commune in 1871 to the fightback of British workers during the New Unionism movement of the 1880s, the victories and the defeats of the time were distilled in Eleanor's political thought, action and commitment.

She was a lover of theatre and performance, undoubtedly helpful in speaking at hundreds of workers' meetings. She was an avid reader and entertainer. She helped bring Ibsen and Flaubert to British audiences, as well as terror to the lives of ruthless bosses in London's East End. She offered up opinions on everything from the American Civil War to Shakespeare.

Revolutionary socialism was always closest to her heart. Karl Marx famously said that while his elder daughter, Jenny, was like him, "Tussy [Eleanor's nickname] *is* me". Her family's, and in particular her father's, commitment to socialism had a huge impact on her life and politics. She spent her teenage years at the congresses of the International Working Men's Association (IWMA), the first international workers' organisation, and spent much of her adult life translating and organising the distribution of Karl Marx's work. But while she continued in his spirit, she also found her own.

At the core of Eleanor Marx's politics was internationalism. At the age of just 16 she looked to Paris and its Commune for what workers – men and women – could do. She committed herself to sharing its history and its lessons. From an early age she stood up for the most downtrodden in society. As a child, she identified with the struggles of Irish republicans, an understanding that would pay off later when it came to organising politicised Irish workers in east London.

She built early socialist organisation in Britain long before the advent of the Labour Party. She campaigned for free speech and the right of activists to organise on the streets.

She recognised the importance of building movements and taking socialist ideas to their centres. As she so brilliantly put it in a speech to the May Day demonstration in 1890: "We must not be like some Christians who sin for six days and go to church on the seventh, but we must speak for the cause daily, and make the men, and especially the women that we meet, come into the ranks to help us" (www.marxists.org/archive/eleanor-marx/works/mayday.htm).

She worked tirelessly to spread the struggles, strikes and lessons of New Unionism – the organisation of the "unorganisable" to fight for an eight-hour day, better pay and improved conditions.

Much has been made in recent years about the changing nature of work and the implications of this for workers' organisation. These are important debates touching on questions of whether certain groups of workers can organise or fight back.

In the 1880s the working lives of matchwomen, gas workers and dockers were every bit as precarious as today's fast food workers or call centre staff, if not more so. They had little or no history of organisation, were excluded from existing unions and were vilified and patronised in equal measure. But they fought and they won. Eleanor organised among these workers across the country and was one of the founders of the National Union of Gas Workers and General Labourers, now the GMB.

She wrote on the workers' movement in Britain and the US and on the terrible working conditions and poverty that workers endured. She was a tribune of the oppressed, organising with and agitating among women and migrant workers in particular, from the women workers of Silvertown to the Jewish tailors of Stepney.

Eleanor wrote and spoke on the issue of women's liberation. During her lifetime the women's movement in Britain was largely dominated by middle class women and their interests. But Eleanor saw women as crucial to the success of the workers' movement and to the emancipation of the working class as a whole, just as she saw the workers' movement and its progress as key to the liberation of women. She didn't reject the gains being made in areas such as women's education, but she recognised early on that working women had more in common with working men than they did with the leaders of the women's rights movement. She argued that, while granting the vote to women was important, voting itself was not enough.

She recognised that women and men had to organise alongside one another. In 1892 she wrote, "And now, what do we women have to do? One thing without any doubt. We will organise – organise not as 'women' but as *proletarians*; not as female rivals of our working men but as their comrades in struggle" (www.marxists.org/archive/draper/1976/women/5-emarx.html).

She impressed with her verve and bravery. The gas workers called her "Our Old Stoker". They and others were constantly impressed with both the delivery and strength of her arguments.

Yet so many accounts of Eleanor's life focus on her troubled personal life and her suicide. There is so much more to her life and legacy than that. Eleanor Marx should be placed where she belongs – at the centre of a powerful workers' movement that changed the nature of British trade unionism and the position of the most exploited and oppressed in society.

★ 2: THE EARLY YEARS

Eleanor Marx was born in January 1855 in Dean Street in Soho, the heart of London and the centre of life for political émigrés. During her early life the family was constantly under the pressure of poverty, with bailiffs regularly at their door.

Three years before Eleanor's birth her family found they could not afford a coffin for their daughter Franziska without taking out a hefty loan. The pressures inevitably took their toll. In 1862 Karl Marx wrote, "Every day my wife tells me she wishes she and the children were dead and buried. And really I cannot argue with her. For the humiliations, torments and terrors that have to be gone through in this situation are really indescribable" (quoted in Alex Callinicos, *The Revolutionary Ideas of Karl Marx*, Bookmarks, 2010, p35).

Despite the pressures of poverty on the Marx family and all of them suffering from some illness or other throughout her childhood, the youngest Marx's early life appears to have been stimulating socially, culturally and, of course, politically.

She had a close relationship with her father. Eleanor spent many of her early years playing next to Karl in his study while he wrote the first volume of *Capital* and her mother, Jenny, tirelessly transcribed it.

Her father was also a talented storyteller and entertained Eleanor both with his own creations and those of famous authors. Eleanor enjoyed the story of Hans Rockle, a fictional poor magician, and learnt German from the stories of the Brothers Grimm. She listened to the works of Homer and to *The Arabian Nights*, and could perform whole passages from Shakespeare (which seems to have been like some sort of family bible) by a young age. Her mother would take the children to see plays in London's West End. This all inspired a passion for literature and theatre that stayed with Eleanor throughout her life.

Eleanor was a bright young woman, despite a lack of formal schooling. Although her older sisters had attended school until they were 14, Eleanor didn't go to school until she was 11, and even then quite sporadically. She found, like many children do, that school got in the way of real life.

The Marx family had to rely hugely on Friedrich Engels, Karl Marx's closest friend and collaborator and a notable theorist in his own right. He provided the financial support that allowed the Marxes to survive. Engels and Eleanor forged a strong relationship throughout her childhood; Eleanor's stamp collecting was one of their first points of correspondence, with Engels generously contributing to her growing collection.

Politics was an early passion. Eleanor followed the American Civil War with particular interest. When she was nine years old, she wrote to Abraham Lincoln because, as she later explained, "I felt absolutely convinced that Abraham Lincoln badly needed my advice as to the war" (quoted in Rachel Holmes, *Eleanor Marx: A Life*, Bloomsbury, 2014, p66). She also displayed great interest in a visit to London of Giuseppe Garibaldi, the Italian republican leader.

When she was 14, Eleanor and Karl Marx visited Engels and his partner, Lizzy Burns, in Manchester. It was here that she developed an interest in Irish politics. Tensions were running high in Manchester at the time following the execution in 1867 of two Irishmen known as the Manchester Martyrs. After a widely discredited tria, they had been sentenced to death for the killing of a police officer during an attempt to free two imprisoned Irish republican leaders.

Karl Marx and Engels were both attempting to understand and explain the Irish nationalist movement. For Eleanor, it was a time of great excitement and education. She describes a day of particularly radical sightseeing with Lizzy who: "showed me the stall where Kelly [the Irish republican leader] sold pots, and the house where he lived" (quoted in Holmes, p93).

On returning to London, Eleanor took her whole family to a demonstration in support of the Fenians, began research for Engels' book on Ireland, wrote to Lizzy in Manchester about ongoing developments and read Irish newspapers. No wonder she signed her letters "Fenian Sister".

But while Irish politics remained an ongoing interest, soon it was events in France that were to become of utmost importance to Eleanor and socialists across the world.

★ 3: THE PARIS COMMUNE

In 1871 Paris rose up. This was a key event that really shaped Eleanor and her politics. She was just 16. Disgust at a bourgeois government that had overthrown an empire but delivered nothing for workers inspired the world's first successful working class revolution.

The Paris Commune only survived for two months, but it was the most democratic and liberating government the world had ever seen. It was led by workers, for workers. It transformed society and to this day provides a crucial alternative model of democracy where power lies in workers' hands.

It is an inspiring period. The Commune did more in 72 days than most reformist governments do in years of office. It pulled thousands out of poverty. It abolished conscription, got rid of the army and introduced the National Guard, which every worker could join.

Arthur Arnould, an elected member of the Commune Council, said that, "during [the Commune's] short reign not a single man, woman, child or old person was hungry, or cold, or homeless... It was amazing to see how with only tiny resources this government...chased famine from the hearths of the huge population... That was one of the miracles of a true democracy" (quoted in Donny Gluckstein, *The*

Paris Commune: A Revolution in Democracy, Haymarket, 2011, pp10-11).

The Paris Commune established the principles that all public officials should be elected, subject to recall and paid workers' wages so there was no interest in misrepresentation.

Karl Marx did not come up with a theory of what real democracy would look like; he learnt it from the Paris Commune. He dedicated one of his most important works, *The Civil War in France*, to the Commune and the lessons that the working class could learn from it. Marx said that this was a "working class government... the political form at last discovered under which to work the economical emancipation of labour", and that "working men's [sic] Paris, with its Commune, will be for ever celebrated as a glorious harbinger of a new society" (quoted in Gluckstein, p185).

But, of course, it wasn't just working men that Paris belonged to. Women were central to fighting for the Commune and it transformed their lives. Equal pay was introduced, divorce rights were granted and girls' education was promoted. There were many female leaders of the Commune, most notably Louise Michel, who argued that women and men not only had an interest in uniting, but that it was crucial to the Commune's success. Women fought alongside men in the defence of the new society and for Eleanor this was crucial. She saw how women could not only improve their own condition, but also how women and men could struggle together to forge a new society.

Eleanor had personal connections with the Commune. A friend at the time was Elisabeth Dmitrieff, co-founder of the Russian section of the First International. Dmitrieff became an envoy to the Commune and organised the women's committees and unions in Paris. And the husband of Eleanor's eldest sister, Laura, was the great Communard Paul Lafargue.

But the Commune was brutally crushed by the French government. Bloody Week followed after just 72 days, leading to the slaughter of some 20,000 Communards and their supporters. Eleanor was visiting Laura in Bordeaux at the time and her brother-in-law, Paul Lafargue, had gone missing.

It was in France that Eleanor had her first brush with the law. The French ruling class were determined to punish all those they saw as supporting the Commune, and the Marxes and Lafargues were high on the list. Eleanor and her sister, Jenny, were interrogated and imprisoned for three days.

Following her return to London, Eleanor threw herself into organising solidarity with the Commune and supporting its refugees. The London Congress of the IWMA was held in September. Much discussion focused on the Commune and its refugees. Eleanor contributed enthusiastically to these discussions. But she also committed herself practically. By the end of 1871 she was beginning to play an important role in the coordination of the Relief Committee for Communards. She raised money for the refugees who made it to England.

Their situation had a profound effect on Eleanor. In a letter to the German revolutionary Wilhelm Liebknecht she wrote, "There are a great many members of the Commune here and the poor refugees suffer frightfully... they have none of them any money and you can't think how difficult it is for them to get work. I wish they'd taken some of the millions they're accused of having stolen" (quoted in Yvonne Kapp, *Eleanor Marx, vol 1: Family Life, 1855-1983*, Virago, 1972, pp133-134).

Exiled Communards were knocking at the Marx family's door. When the Commune was finally crushed, the last to leave the last barricade was a man called Prosper-Olivier Lissagaray. He escaped to England and found his way to the Marx house (as so many revolutionary refugees did). He was Eleanor's first serious partner.

Lissagaray later wrote and published a book about the Commune and his experiences. Eleanor became his main researcher and translator. *History of the Paris Commune* was to be the translation that made the real experience accessible to thousands and remains one of the great writings on the Commune.

Not everyone was as admiring of the Communards. Within the IWMA itself there was a split over support for them and the emphasis placed on the activity of workers themselves. Until 1871, the idea of workers' self-emancipation had remained pretty abstract, even to Marx himself.

For years afterwards Eleanor organised and spoke at the annual Commune anniversary meeting. In these speeches she returned to the question of the role of women. At the 1885 anniversary meeting, for example, Rachel Holmes describes how "she made the central role of women in the Paris Commune and socialism the subject of her speech. This was the first time women's leadership of the Commune was the subject of an anniversary address" (Holmes, p256).

Eleanor was learning important lessons. The experience of the Commune gave her a vision of a socialist society where the working class could organise and take control of their own lives. She saw for the first time that things could be different. This had a fundamental impact on her for the rest of her life.

★ 4: THE BUSIEST DECADE

The 1880s were the most significant decade in Eleanor Marx's life. The early part of the decade brought some important turning points in her personal life. In 1881 her mother died of cancer. By the end of 1883 both her elder sister, Jenny, and her father were dead.

The relationships with her mother and sister were close ones. But it was the relationship with her father that shaped her most of all. For a long time she had been an important contributor to his political work, acting as his secretary and researcher. The deaths also marked an important change in her ability to strike out on her own. She took charge of her father's papers and set to work compiling his notes and organising the translation of his work. She also met Edward Aveling, a man with whom she would have a political and (often fraught) personal relationship for the rest of her life.

Politically, this was the decade in which Eleanor was to become an important player at a time of rapid change. For decades the working class and its organisations had been largely dormant. Writing in 1895, Eleanor describes how: "For years the political movement of the workers as a class was, if not dead, at least in a profound sleep" (www.marxists.org/archive/eleanor-marx/1895/working-class-england/ch01.htm).

The time was ripe for new ideas about how society should be organised. There had been years of repression in Ireland and a recession that brought an end to Victorian prosperity. There were huge gaps between rich and poor.

Engels wrote of the majority of workers in London and other cities living in: "an ever spreading pool...of misery and desolation, of starvation when out of work, and degradation, physical and moral, when in work" (quoted in Yvonne Kapp, *Eleanor Marx, vol 2: The Crowded Years, 1884-1898*, Virago, 1976, p48). Just as today, imperial adventures and terrible exploitation had the potential to make workers question the status quo.

Industrial struggle hadn't completely disappeared since the end of the Chartist movement some 30 years earlier. There had been strikes across the country and in a range of industries. But these were largely fought by the craft unions, organisations which represented those in "skilled" work, most of whom would have completed an apprenticeship. They were interested in a particular group of workers rather than big political questions or furthering the interests of the working class as a whole.

The women's movement, where Eleanor's other interests lay, was similarly limited. During Eleanor's lifetime ideas about women focused largely on their role as wives and mothers. If, as Eleanor believed, the ruling ideas of society are the ideas of the ruling class, the ruling class wanted women in the home.

In the women's movement important campaigns were in progress, including around women's access to education and for the vote. But the movement was dominated by middle class women, who were at best philanthropic and at worst downright contemptuous towards working class women.

Working class women had never been absent from the kind of mass movements that Eleanor advocated and built. Indeed, women had been involved in many of the working class struggles of the early 19th century, from mass struggles in the textile industry through Chartism to the struggle around Irish independence.

During Chartism women had signed the petitions in their thousands, marched in the demonstrations and spoken on public platforms. Women were also widely involved in the mass flying pickets that brought people out of the factories in 1842. Working class women in areas where they had industrial strength were particularly radical. When one of those responsible for repressing the 1848 risings in Europe visited Britain in 1850, he had to run for his life from a Chartist crowd. A contemporary newspaper describes how a "large portion of females took part in this glorious manifestation, and tore the fellow's grisly moustachios until he roared again and again with pain and fury" (*Reynold's Weekly Newspaper*, 8 September 1850).

However, there had been a general decline in the level of activism among the whole working class, including women. Many of the organisations that replaced the former militant activist campaigns were biased against women and working class men too. Craft unions, for example, were almost exclusively male, though they also excluded the vast majority of working class men. Where women's trade union organisations existed, they were craft unions and the leadership was the preserve of middle class women such as Clementina Black, the secretary of the Women's Trade Union League.

Working class men and women, while being largely ignored by the craft unions, were similarly ignored by the main political parties. Parliamentary politics was dominated by two main parties: the Liberals and the Tories. Women and nearly half of all men could not vote.

Thousands of young workers had moved to growing towns and cities to live and work. The population of London's West Ham, where numerous workplaces were based and where Eleanor focused much of her organising, grew tenfold between the 1851 and 1891 censuses. Increasing industrialisation meant this was replicated in cities across the country.

Stark social divisions emerged. The bourgeoisie built what Annie Besant, the Fabian journalist, described as their "'mansions and pleasure grounds' on the labour of those who inhabited the 'reeking slums within the sound of the factory bells'" (Louise Raw, *Striking a Light: The Bryant and May Matchwomen and their Place in History*, Continuum, p37).

Poverty was rife. Work conditions were hazardous. And insanitary conditions and overcrowding led to recurring outbreaks of diseases such as cholera and tuberculosis.

In the 1880s Eleanor began to witness the poverty of London's East End for herself. She described what she saw in letter after letter. For example, in 1887 she wrote, "To walk through the streets is heartrending. I know the East End well, and I know people who have lived there for years... Thousands who usually can just keep going at any rate during the first months of the winter are this year starving" (Holmes, p301).

This combination of increasing poverty, a recession taking hold, political issues bubbling under the surface and a lack of representation for working class people helped shape the decade.

During the 1880s Eleanor Marx worked as a teacher, typist and researcher. She translated Gustave Flaubert's *Madam Bovary* and Henrik Ibsen's *A Doll's House* (learning Norwegian along the way). She organised the translation of her father's great work *Capital* and travelled to the US and Europe. But she dedicated most of her attention to her political work as an organiser and agitator. It was to be her busiest decade.

★ 5: TRANSITION YEARS

In the early 1880s socialist organisation was beginning to develop in Britain. Eleanor was to be central to it and crucial in shaping its direction. In 1881, the Democratic Federation was initiated by a number of socialists and left wing liberals.

It was led by Henry Hyndman. Initially it focused on land reform — a campaign that attracted many Irish workers — and unemployment on the land. Sharp political differences quickly emerged: "Gladstone's policy of coercion towards Ireland evoked an outraged response in the Federation. It participated in a massive anti-government demonstration in Hyde Park. A large section of radicals withdrew from the new body because of its antagonism to the Liberal government. This made the way clearer for the socialists," (John Charlton, *It Just Went Like Tinder*, Redwords, 1999, p65).

By 1884 it had changed its name to the Social Democratic Federation (SDF). Eleanor joined and began building the new organisation, believing that it was crucial to deliver meaningful and effective solidarity to striking workers and also to bring socialist ideas to the mass movement. Both she and Edward Aveling were elected to the SDF executive and helped shape its new explicitly socialist programme. She was especially diligent, attending every executive meeting and organising street meetings and demonstrations. The SDF began to employ new ways of communicating with working class people. For example, when the usual outlets wouldn't sell the SDF's newspaper *Justice*, members began to sell it on the streets.

Initially, the organisation was successful. It was joined by the Labour Emancipation League, a socialist club based in east London, and began to make connections with this important area. It was also beginning to emerge as a viable force at a national level, with branches in Newcastle and Liverpool and supporters from Bristol to Edinburgh.

Although certain leaders of the SDF saw strikes primarily as a place for socialist agitation rather than as central to class struggle, they began to connect with a wider audience of working class people. Hassan Mahamdallie explains how, for example: "The receptiveness of active groups of workers to Marxism was demonstrated by the setting up of a branch in Blackburn after intervention in the 1884 cotton strike" (Hassan Mahamdallie, *Crossing the 'River of Fire': the Socialism of William Morris*, Redwords, 2008, p46).

But by 1884 the SDF's leadership were experiencing irreconcilable differences. Eleanor, a driving force behind the move, was joined by Aveling and other leading socialists such as William Morris and Ernest Belfort Bax, in setting up the Socialist League, which they formed as a challenge to the SDF's elitist and nationalist outlook.

Henry Hyndman's attitudes were a primary cause of the split. He was a frock-coated former Tory who held on to many backward ideas. Eleanor and Hyndman had history: he had invited both Eleanor and her father to his house to engage them in discussions around the setting up of the Democratic Federation. Both father and daughter were unimpressed with his approach from the outset, particularly his incredibly patronising attitude towards workers themselves. Hyndman believed that "a slave cannot be freed by the slaves themselves". He argued that "the leadership, the initiative, the teaching, the organisation must come from those who are born into a different position and are trained to use their faculties in early life" (quoted in Holmes, pp141-142).

He was convinced that socialism was to be preached to the masses without them taking agency for themselves. For Eleanor and her comrades, workers' self-agency was always at the centre of their approach. She didn't believe in simply preaching socialism to workers. She wanted to link Marxist ideas with the day-to-day lives and political activity of working people.

Hyndman was known for being nationalistic, jingoistic and anti-Semitic. Eleanor wrote to Wilhelm Liebknecht at the start of 1885: "One of our chief points of conflict with Hyndman is that whereas we wish to make this a really international movement...Mr Hyndman, whenever he could do so with impunity, has endeavoured to set English workmen against 'foreigners'" (quoted in Kapp, vol 2, p59).

Nationalism was described by Eleanor and her Socialist League comrades as the "persistent foe of Socialists". Inspired by the Paris Commune, talking to immigrant workers in London, in contact with numerous international socialists and herself the daughter of immigrants, internationalism was hugely important to her.

Another reason for the rift was Hyndman's attitude to the left of the Liberal Party. William Morris described Hyndman's "perpetual sneers at, and abuse of the Radicals" (Mahamdallie, p48). Morris — and Eleanor — rightly asserted that, although the political differences between socialists and radicals were clear, they were an important group to work with in the movements and often a receptive audience for socialist ideas.

Eleanor's enduring relationship with Engels was especially important during the setting up of the Socialist League. Engels recognised Eleanor as a gifted organiser with a talented theoretical mind. He wrote, "The whole movement here is but a phantom, but if it is possible to draw into the Socialist League a kernel of people who have a good theoretical understanding, much will be gained for a genuine mass movement, which will not long be coming" (Mahamdallie, p49).

Eleanor began to write extensively in the Socialist League's newspaper, *Commonweal*, edited by William Morris. Her internationalism was particularly prominent; she took responsibility for the section entitled "Record of the Revolutionary International Movement", reporting news from socialists across the world.

There was significant overlap between the SDF and Socialist League for the rest of the decade. They were often in competition with one another. Both organisations were developing good relationships with young workers such as Ben Tillett, Tom Mann and Will Thorne — all talented militants rooted in the working class who became central to the development of the New Unions later in the decade.

Both organisations remained relatively small throughout the 1880s. While they connected with workers and became important leaders in the movements and strikes that were to come, a legacy of propagandising often held strong. Infighting, however important the debates were, sometimes left them behind. In short, these were new and sometimes challenging times for socialists and new questions were being raised. Many socialists were central to the workers' movement despite their organisations, not because of them. Over the coming years Eleanor was to move between the two organisations and her own branch, the Bloomsbury Socialist Society.

Socialists were debating big questions, often for the first time. Within the Socialist League arguments quickly began to take place. Firstly, there were tensions on the issue of parliamentary representation and even voting at all. Eleanor and her grouping believed that these issues were ones the Socialist League had to have something to say about or risk becoming purely a propagandist organisation or, worse, a reading group. Eleanor was particularly vitriolic about the anarchist section who condemned engagement with electoral issues, strikes and improvements in workers' conditions as mere "palliatives" (Mahamdallie, p93).

But political street movements were beginning to move into action. Despite — or perhaps spurred on by — the debates within socialist organisations, Eleanor was to throw herself into these movements and attempt to link Marxism with the situation of working class people.

★ 6:
THE
WOMAN
QUESTION

In 1886 Eleanor Marx published *The Woman Question from a Socialist Point of View* with Edward Aveling. This important pamphlet contributed to debates in both the women's movement and the workers' movement. It explained the position of women in society and engaged with a number of contemporary issues. But it also aimed to explain the steps that needed to be taken by both movements to achieve real women's liberation.

It was a critique of capitalism as a system that places an extra burden on women, and working class women in particular, and that distorts relationships and sexuality. Although the latter half of the title was often omitted on republication throughout the 20th century, the pamphlet included a radical vision of a socialist society.

Debates were raging about the role of women in society and those on the right and left were taking up "the woman question". Eleanor Marx and Edward Aveling wanted to contribute to a Marxist understanding of women's oppression.

Friedrich Engels had taken up the question of women's oppression in his book *The Origin of the Family, Private Property and the State*, written just two years before. *The Woman Question from a Socialist Point of View*, although purportedly a reply to August Bebel's *Women and Socialism*, was as much about building on Engels' work in which he makes the class roots of women's oppression explicit.

Like Engels, Eleanor and Aveling recognised that "the woman question is one of the organisation of society as a whole". But they noted that the dominant strand within the women's movement was of reform, not revolution. The women's movement was dominated by "excellent and hard-working folk who agitate for that perfectly just aim, woman suffrage; for the repeal of the Contagious Diseases Act...for the higher education of women; for the opening to them of universities, the learned professions, and all callings, from that of teacher to that of bagman."

Eleanor and Aveling recognised that those campaigning for these reforms were "of the well-to-do classes, as a rule" and the results "palliative, not remedial". Eleanor herself had been involved in some of these campaigns, supporting middle class female candidates in London School Board elections, for example, and as a teacher, she recognised the importance of girls' and women's education. But in the pamphlet she argues that these campaigns did not go far enough.

A downturn in struggle had affected both women and men, and the pamphlet aimed to encourage a fightback. By linking "the woman question" to the labour and socialist movements, she aimed to give a clear direction. The pamphlet argued that class was central to women's liberation, but it did not ignore the sexism that women experienced.

For example, the pamphlet addresses the issue of prostitution not from a moral perspective but from a political one. Eleanor had been writing on the issue for some time, but here she addresses squarely the role of capitalism: "To get rid of prostitution, we must get rid of the social conditions that are its parent. Midnight meetings, refuges for the distressed, all the well-meant attempts to grapple with this awful problem are, as their initiators despairingly admit, futile... Get rid of this, the capitalistic system of production, say the Socialists, and prostitution will pass away."

Eleanor placed the blame firmly at the feet of the ruling class: "The truth, not fully recognised even by those anxious to do good to woman, is that she, like the labour-classes, is in an oppressed condition; that her position, like theirs, is one of merciless degradation. Women are the creatures of an organised tyranny of men, as the workers are the creatures of an organised tyranny of idlers. Even where this much is grasped, we must never be weary of insisting on the non-understanding that for women, as for the labouring classes, no solution of the difficulties and problems that present themselves is really possible in the present condition of society... Both the oppressed classes, women and the immediate producers, must understand that their emancipation will come from themselves."

In *The Woman Question from a Socialist Point of View* Eleanor and Aveling adopt a formulation that seems to use oppression and exploitation interchangeably. They do not appear to make a distinction between the economic extract of surplus value and systematic social discrimination. But they argue that working class women and bourgeois women experience sexism differently and have different priorities.

For Eleanor, Marxism helped to explain the basis of women's oppression and the basis for getting rid of it.

She argued that nothing was permanent and that both oppression and exploitation were "only certain temporary conventions of society, like the convention that French is the language of diplomacy".

The pamphlet concludes with a vision of an alternative society that delivers for women and men: "The State under Socialism, if indeed a word of such ugly historical associations is retained, will be the organised capacity of a community of workers. Its officials will be no better and no worse off than their fellows. The divorce between art and labour, the antagonism between head and hand work, that grieves the souls of artists, without their knowing in most cases the economic cause of their grief, will vanish."

Eleanor's position appears to become clearer over the next ten years, presumably as a result of the political movements and industrial struggles she was involved in. In 1892 Eleanor was specially commissioned by German socialist Luise Kautsky to write four articles for an Austrian women's paper. These addressed the question of how women should organise and reported on how English working women were organising in trade unions. She wrote, "Now, it seems to me that we must commence by organising as trade-unionists using our united strength as a means of reaching the ultimate goal, the emancipation of our class. The job will not be easy. In fact, the conditions of female labour are such that it is often heartbreakingly difficult to make progress. But from day to day the job will become easier, and it will begin to look less and less difficult in proportion as the women and especially the men learn to see what strength lies in the unification of all workers" (www.marxists.org/archive/draper/1976/women/5-emarx.html).

In 1896 she wrote a report in *Justice*, the SDF's newspaper, about the Social Democratic Party of Germany's Gotha Congress. She places particular emphasis on the speech of Clara Zetkin, the German Marxist and later founder of International Women's Day. Zetkin made an important contribution to ongoing debates and a Marxist understanding of women's oppression. She argued that while bourgeois women were competing with bourgeois men, working class women were not held down by working class men. She asserted that their interests lie together. Eleanor quotes Zetkin: "And that is why the working woman cannot be like the bourgeois woman who has to fight against the man of her own class... With the proletarian women, on the contrary, it is a struggle of the woman *with* the man of her own class against the capitalist class... Her end and aim are not the right of free competition with men, but to obtain the political power of the proletariat."

Eleanor Marx, in her report on Zetkin's speech, recognises something important. The position of working class women is "not merely reactionary, it is also revolutionary".

★ 7: THE US TOUR

In 1886 Eleanor Marx, along with Edward Aveling and the German Social Democrat Wilhelm Leibknicht, undertook a four-month tour of the US. It was to provide an eye-opening comparison for Eleanor and became the subject of a substantial pamphlet on her return, published in 1888. They visited some 35 towns and cities from New York to Kansas City and many in between.

The US, like Britain, was in a state of flux. While the government and big business attempted to exert control following the Civil War, millions of US workers were taking up radical ideas. Like Britain, there had been limited industrial struggle throughout much of the 19th century. But things were taking a different turn. Great movements, industrial and political, were in progress throughout the 1880s. Howard Zinn describes it as a time when "revolutionary organizations existed in major American cities, and revolutionary talk was in the air" (Howard Zinn, *A People's History of the United States*, Harper Perennial Modern Classics, 2005, p265).

Migrants were arriving from Germany, Italy and Greece as well as Ireland and Eastern Europe, just like London; over 5 million migrants entered the US in the 1880s. These workers were having an influence on the socialist movement, despite the bosses trying to use them to undercut other workers.

The Working-Class Movement in America, written by Eleanor in collaboration with Aveling, opens with an assessment of the US working class movement based on a long (but by no means exhaustive) list of radical publications. It was not just the number of organisations that impressed them, but the level of class consciousness displayed by US workers.

They describe how, "In England, to a large extent, the attempt to make the workers believe that there is a community of interests between them and their employers still succeeds... But in America this mutual deception is nearly at an end. The working men and the capitalists in the majority of cases quite understand that each, as a class, is the deadly and inexorable foe of the other."

Tensions were high. Four months before Eleanor's arrival, a demonstration of 3,000 in Chicago had become a turning point; it became known as the Haymarket Affair. A bomb had been detonated on a workers' demonstration (possibly by an agent provocateur) resulting in clashes between the police and protesters. One person was killed and many were wounded. The police arrested eight anarchist leaders in Chicago, only one of whom had been on the demonstration. They were sentenced to death.

This miscarriage of justice was a hot topic and Eleanor engaged with it in her speeches and in writing. She attacked the lies of the ruling class and drew particular attention to the role of the media in demonising the protesters. She wrote articles for British newspapers that called for solidarity from workers across the world.

Eleanor visited Chicago as part of the tour and spoke at a number of meetings. What is most impressive is her ability to show support for the Chicago anarchists while not suppressing her differences.

In one of her speeches she said, "I should feel I was neglecting a manifest duty, if I did not refer to a matter which I am sure is present in the minds and hearts of all here tonight; which is present in the minds and hearts of all honest men and women. I mean, of course, to the anarchist trial – it is called a trial – and a condemnation to death of seven men. Now I do not hesitate to say most emphatically and explicitly that if that sentence is carried out, it will be one of the most infamous legal murders that has ever been perpetrated. The execution of these men would be neither more nor less than murder. I am no anarchist, but I feel all the more that I am bound to say this" (quoted in Kapp, vol 2, p161).

But this didn't mean she shied away from debates between anarchists and socialists. *The Working-Class Movement in America* pointed out that while both socialists and anarchists attacked capitalism, "the Anarchist attacks it from the individualist, conservative, reactionary point of view." Although she always recognised that a miscarriage of justice had been done, she was uncompromising about what she saw as an approach that didn't deliver. As Rachel Holmes puts it, "from the beginning of their 'agitation' tour of America, Eleanor had encouraged her audiences to 'throw three bombs amongst the masses: agitation, education and organisation'" (Holmes, p285).

Despite the repression of workers' organisation, struggle continued. In 1886 there were over 1,400 strikes involving half a million workers. The overarching campaign, just like the one being developed in Britain, was for an eight-hour day.

Women were also organising. Eleanor Marx was impressed by their action. In 1884 female textile workers had gone on strike. In 1885 shirt makers in New York, men and women together, had gone on strike. They won higher wages and shorter hours. In the Knights of Labor, a union federation, there were 50,000 female members in nearly 200 women's assemblies. Women leaders were emerging, such as Leonora Barry, an Irish woman who had emigrated to the US and became "master workman" of her assembly.

Eleanor returned to the question of organising women in her final speech in US on 23 December. She argued that working women in the US (who she considered to be in an even worse position than those in Britain) should organise not separately but as part of the workers' movement as a whole.

She drew inspiration and lessons from workers in the US during one of the most important periods for its working class movement. And Eleanor herself made a lasting impression. During the 1930s the meeting place of the Chicago branch of the Scandinavian Workers League was named the Eleanor Marx Women's Club.

★ 8:
THE
MOVEMENTS

The year 1885 was particularly busy for Eleanor Marx. Following the death of General Gordon at the hands of the Sudanese in January, the press and politicians went all out against those opposed to the British Empire.

Eleanor helped to organise a meeting against the war in Sudan and contributed to an impressive pamphlet against imperialism. It laid out the socialist case against imperialism, arguing that war was solely for the purposes of the expansion of capitalism and had no benefits to the people of Africa.

It continued with "we ask you to consider who it is that have to do the fighting on this and similar occasions. Is it the market-hunting class themselves? Is it they who form the rank and file of the army? No! But the sons and brothers of the working classes at home... They it is who conquer, for the wealthy middle and upper classes, new lands for exploitation, fresh populations for pillage" (quoted in Holmes, pp241-242).

This was 30 years before the First World War. For an organisation that had yet to witness the needless slaughter of millions of working class people in imperialist conflict, it was remarkably far-sighted.

But this stand, however impressive, did not rally the British working class. It was the issue of police repression that saw remarkable demonstrations of strength.

Socialists — now that their ideas were being taken up by many people — began to experience police repression. Their stalls were stopped and the International Club in central London was attacked by the police. The state was obviously beginning to be shaken by the traction of socialist ideas.

Radicals and socialists, many in the new socialist organisations, were roughed up. When they moved their meetings to the docklands in east London, they were charged with causing an obstruction — the police's go-to charge for stopping street demonstrations both then and ever since. Socialists were arrested and fined every week. This spurred on the movement. In September 1885, the week following a crackdown on Dod Street in Limehouse, 50,000 people arrived for an outdoor meeting. Eleanor Marx was one of the speakers at that demonstration. It is impressive for socialists — in new, changing organisations too — to pull this number of people around them in such a visible way.

Running alongside the Free Speech campaign was a movement of unemployed workers who were becoming increasingly visible. In February 1886 a demonstration in Trafalgar Square included speeches from socialist speakers. John Burns, an SDF member and later a leader in the New Unionism movement, led the demonstration through the West End. The protest was attacked by the rich — verbally by the gentlemen standing at the side of the road and quite literally by the servants who threw stones at the demonstrators. The unemployed workers retaliated by smashing up shops and clubs.

There were increasing mobilisations around Ireland. On Easter Sunday 1887 there was a demonstration of

150,000 people to protest against the Crimes Bill, a law to remove the rights of many Irish tenants fighting evictions in their homeland.

Irish workers in London and across Britain were at the bottom of the heap. Eleanor's early and continuing interest in Irish independence, arguably the most persistent area of controversy in British politics for a century, stood her in good stead throughout these years.

Large numbers of Irish people worked in the "unskilled" trades of dock work, match work and the gas industry; the strike register of the matchwomen's strike of 1888, for example, lists many Irish names. Social commentators from Henry Mayhew to Charles Booth often disparagingly reported the high number of Irish immigrants in the neighbourhoods around the workplaces most affected (Raw, pp174-190). Many of these workers identified with various Irish causes from Repeal of the Act of Union to the land struggles, to British repression and the constitutional disputes that eventually led to Home Rule.

The Irish were a target audience for radicals and socialists throughout the period, and 1887 marked a year of huge mobilisations and considerable disorder in London over the Irish situation. Branches of socialist organisations were recorded in many areas of high Irish population and *Commonweal* and *Justice* (publications of the Socialist League and the SDF respectively) both record mobilisation points for demonstrations in Irish areas such as Canning Town, Poplar, Limehouse and Shadwell (*Justice*, 13 July 1888).

The growth of these movements and the role of socialists within them were an important background to the industrial upsurge that was about to explode. For Eleanor, linking the political to the economic was vital. She saw the importance of political struggles in giving confidence to workers to fight the bosses and the government.

★ 9: THE BIRTH OF NEW UNIONISM

For years small groups of people in Britain had talked about socialism. In 1888 they found themselves at the centre of an explosion of mass struggle. The year signalled the birth of New Unionism and of the modern trade union movement. And Eleanor threw herself into the new movement, agitating, organising and speaking across the country.

New Unionism was the movement of previously unorganised workers into trade union organisation and activity. Britain – and London in particular – was gripped by this new fever. From the Bryant and May matchwomen to the Great Dock Strike via many other unrecorded struggles, it involved tens of thousands of workers, manifesting itself in mass strikes and protests across the country. It was, according to Engels, "the movement of the greatest promise" to emerge in years (www.marxists.org/archive/marx/works/1889/08/26.htm).

New Unionism changed everything. As well as involving workers who had little or no experience of trade union militancy, it also gave a voice to the most downtrodden in society: precarious workers, women and migrants. For years workers had received awful pay and experienced terrible conditions in the workplace. Their work was casual, their labour apparently disposable. After years of limited industrial struggle there was a spark of resistance. In the summer of 1888 around 1,400 women workers at the Bryant and May match factory in Bow, east London, walked out on strike.

The inspiring matchwomen's strike is one of the best documented examples of women's trade union activity at this time and of New Unionism in general. It is a struggle that encapsulated many of the outstanding features of New Unionism, such as the fight against poor conditions and the organisation of previously unorganised workers.

Many of the matchwomen were Irish and their strike is particularly inspiring when you consider the racism they faced and the attempts to scapegoat them. Even before the matchwomen the early stevedores' union on the London waterfront was "manned and officered by the London Irish" with at least a third of strikers' names being Irish and strikes often being organised out of Irish pubs (Charlton, p89). The Irish were a group that was fighting back as workers and receiving solidarity from socialists and radicals throughout the period.

Bad pay was one of the main grievances for the matchwomen working at Bryant and May. Even in comparison to the wages of other women factory workers they were incredibly poorly paid and mercilessly exploited. *Commonweal* describes how they were being "fined for various causes, not always being told what for, and were even made to pay for the brushes with which the factory floors were swept" (*Commonweal*, "Strike of the Matchmakers", 14 July 1888).

Louise Raw's 2011 book *Striking a Light: The Bryant and May Matchwomen and their Place in History* has made a significant and important contribution to understanding the strike. The Bryant and May strike has often been seen as taking place thanks to the efforts of Annie Besant, rather than being inspired by the workers themselves. Besant wrote a piece in the newspaper *The Link* entitled "White Slavery in London", which has long been credited with prompting the women to strike. But, as Raw explains, "Besant explicitly stated at the same time that unionisation would be counterproductive." Besant writes, "Suppose a union was formed (at Bryant and May's), and the girls went on strike: the foreman would simply announce that so many hands were required at so much an hour, and their doors would be besieged within hours" (Raw, p226).

She was wrong. The workers organised themselves, stayed out for three weeks, won their demands and formed a union. The following year the leaders of New Unionism took the matchwomen's example to the docks and gasworks.

Eleanor's approach was radically different to that of Besant. She recognised the importance of workers' self-activity but also the role of socialists within those movements. The inspiration of the matchwomen and thousands of women workers struggling across the country gave her new impetus for the next year in particular, and for the years to come.

★ 10: IN SILVERTOWN

The year 1889 brought New Unionism to the fore and Eleanor Marx was a central player in its success that year. It started with the gas workers. The first significant dispute that year was at the Beckton Gas Works in London's East Ham in March.

The management of the Beckton Gas Works had recently introduced new machinery which worsened the conditions of the men working there. However, the dispute took on much more than that.

Will Thorne started to organise. Thorne was a long-standing member of the Canning Town branch of the SDF and an experienced militant. He had spent years agitating. He described New Unionism as "the culmination of long years of socialist propaganda amongst the underpaid and oppressed workers" (quoted in Kapp, vol 2, p323). He and Eleanor became friends and comrades. Later in life, Thorne was to remark that it was not just Eleanor's political nous that was so useful, but also her practical help, teaching him to read, write and look after the books.

Demanding an eight-hour working day, the gas workers were successful in achieving their demands even without a strike. A wave of strikes across the country also garnered results in places such as Leeds, Bristol, Sunderland, Nottingham, Sheffield, Bury and many more.

On the back of this activism, the National Union of Gas Workers and General Labourers was formed on

12 March 1889 at a meeting in Canning Town called by Will Thorne, Eleanor and others. Yvonne Kapp describes its great success and rapid expansion: "It was received with such acclaim that 800 men joined this nascent union on the spot, tossing their 1s. entrance fee into a bucket. Within a fortnight, though no subscription cards, none but the most rudimentary constitution and no elected executive were yet in being, there were 3,000 members" (Kapp, vol 2, p318).

The growing union included women's branches, set up and organised by Eleanor in October 1889 during the strike at the India-Rubber, Gutta-Percha & Telegraph Works (more commonly known as Silver's) in West Ham. John Tully's book *Silvertown: The Lost Story of a Strike that Shook London and Helped Launch the Modern Labour Movement* (Lawrence & Wishart, 2014) brings the strike to life. He describes how, taking inspiration from the gas workers and the dockers, "Silver's own enormous factory would also be strikebound, the rubber, telegraph, and electrical workers inspired by the dock struggle that was unfolding almost literally on their doorsteps" (Tully, p26).

Nearly 15 percent of Silver's workers were women. Admitting women into the new union marked a significant shift and an example not only of Eleanor's own political strength and dedication, but also of the political strength and dedication of the workers involved.

Eleanor argued consistently for the need for unity, not just between skilled and unskilled workers in unions, but between men and women too. Mark Hutchins and Will Thorne, the president and secretary respectively, laid out the union's interest in women workers, stating that "our Union is also one of the very few in which men and women are on equal terms" (Mark Hutchins and Will Thorne, *The Gas-Workers' Strike, 1889*, July 1890).

They mention, most significantly, the importance of the women's branches within the union and the men's response to their female counterparts: "Mrs Aveling [Eleanor Marx] started a Women's Union at Silvertown, and asked if they would be admitted... 3,000 men were present and her question was answered unanimously and enthusiastically in the affirmative. Since this, female branches — and very flourishing ones — have been organised in London and Bristol...men and women are on equal footing (Hutchins and Thorne, 1890). This approach represented a significant shift in trade unionism. Workers were throwing off the shackles of the old unionism and it was bringing them success.

Socialists and their ideas began to shape the new unions. Eleanor's work, although often ignored by many of her contemporaries, did not go unnoticed by socialists internationally. Laura Lafargue, Eleanor's sister, had a report from Clara Zetkin when she visited her in Paris. Zetkin gave Laura "news of Tussy [Eleanor Marx] whose agitation she is very enthusiastic about, especially her getting up on tables and chairs to harangue the Silvertown women strikes" (Tully, pp122-123).

As well as jumping on tables at meetings, Eleanor committed herself to the more mundane tasks that were required. Ben Tillett, a New Union leader, described how she did "the drudgery of clerical work as well as more responsible duties", while Tom Mann said she was someone who, "possessing a complete mastery of economics... was able, alike in conversation and on a public platform, to hold her own with the best" (Tully, p123).

A local newspaper described how: "She...appealed strongly to the women. They must form unions and work in harmony with the men's trade unions. As the dock strike had taught them the lesson that skilled and unskilled labour should work together, so the present strike should teach them a further great lesson, that they could only win by men and women working in combination. The capitalist was using women to underwork men and that would be the case until women refused to undersell their brothers and husbands" (*Stratford Express*, 9 October, 1889, quoted in Tully p124). Solidarity and unity were Eleanor's watchwords.

★ 11: THE GREAT DOCK STRIKE AND THE JEWISH TAILORS

The tens of thousands of people who worked along the Thames could not fail to notice the gains made by the matchwomen in 1888 and the gas workers in early 1889. The Great Dock Strike of 1889 represents New Unionism's most significant action, involving thousands of workers in east London. An estimated 150,000 families relied on port work in the 1880s. It was mostly casual, with just 10 percent of workers having permanent and regular employment (Charlton, p32).

Beginning in Poplar in mid-August before spreading up and down the river and into other trades, the strike involved 37,000 workers by 22 August. By 25 August there were an estimated 130,000 strikers involved, including ship painters, carpenters and workers in largely female trades such as jam, biscuit and match manufacturing (Raw, p166).

There were hundreds of workplaces, large and small, including the docks themselves and riverside factories and wharves. These spread from the City of London right out to Beckton in the east.

It is worth noting too that many of those who were gas workers also worked in the industries alongside the docks. The demand for gas varied dramatically between winter and summer. Therefore, the demand for gas workers increased massively as winter approached. This meant there was a considerable overlap between those who took part in the gas workers' dispute and the Great Dock Strike. Equally, workers in different industries often lived in the same slums, were members of the same families and came from the same areas of origin in Ireland, Scotland and the rest of England.

These workers were often deemed "unskilled". They were anything but. In gas work, for instance, workers had to contend with numerous hazards and often for very long days and nights. The drive to profit through the use of new machinery made for very skilled and tiring work.

Ben Tillett described how sometimes the struggle to get work became violent, how "coats, flesh, and even ears were torn off... The strong literally threw themselves over the heads of their fellows" (quoted in Charlton, p32). Eleanor herself described scenes at the docks: "The men fight and push and hustle like beasts — not men — and all to earn at best 3d or 4d an hour! So serious has the struggle become that the 'authorities' have had to replace certain iron pailings with wooden ones — the weaker men got impaled in the crush!"(Kapp, vol 2, p263).

As well as the female branches of Eleanor's gas workers' union, women were continuously involved in New Unionism and the Great Dock Strike in particular. Women showed their support in visible ways. During a demonstration of some 10,000 workers marching through the City, the procession stopped to encourage some scabs to stop work. *Commonweal* reported that "on their not complying, groans and execrations burst from the crowd, the women being the loudest" (William Morris, "The Great Strike at the Docks", *Commonweal*, 24 August 1889). Raw also notes further support for the dock strike among women workers: "Female participation in the strike was again demonstrated when 150 tinplate workers, 'mostly girls', came out in solidarity, and 'when a procession of dock labourers passed [them]...they followed in the rear, singing and dancing and playing mouth-organs" (Raw, p167). Women also declared a rent strike on the Commercial Road in Shadwell and produced a banner attacking the landlords that was strung across the road.

During the Dock Strike, Eleanor played an important role behind the scenes. She undertook much of the administration during the strike. This was more than just background work; it was a critical task to organise support for thousands of strikers and their families while employers were trying to force them back to work. A newspaper report of the time describes how Eleanor Marx and local women "work in the interests of the strikers, some 16 or 17 hours a day" (*The Times*, 5 September 1889).

As well as arguing for the involvement of women in New Unionism, Eleanor Marx and other socialists argued for the importance of solidarity and self-organisation. The move away from "up on high" preaching of socialist ideas towards on the ground organisation was a radical departure from the norms of British socialism at the time. As Thorne wrote, "Politics had been preached to them, vague indefinite appeals to revolution, but we offered them something tangible, a definite, clearly-lighted road out of their misery" (quoted in Kapp, vol 2, p323).

Workers were beginning to organise and see real change being made. In West Ham, and many other industrial centres across the country, the dominant form of industry was that of large factories and associated workplaces. Further west in Stepney and Poplar, the make-up of the working class population and the nature of their work were different yet equally exploitative. The workers here were to become involved in New Unionism too.

The Jewish tailors' strike of September 1889 was big and militant. Here the workplace was the workshop of a few dozen workers rather than a huge factory on the riverside. More than 6,000 workers took part and some 120 workshops were shut down. Their demands were, like the gas workers, for a shorter day, and like the dockers, an increase in pay. The Jewish tailors also had to contend with working in relatively isolated small workshops with different and uneven conditions. The strikers, male and female workers, combined and won their demands.

Eleanor's involvement in the Jewish tailors' strike and the movement that surrounded it is another example of her commitment to being a champion of the oppressed. She learnt Yiddish to help her communicate with these workers and spoke on many demonstrations and at strike meetings. For Eleanor, the workers' movement was not just for British workers, or even only British and Irish workers, but for all those who wanted to fight back. Her experience organising largely Irish workers and her socialist grounding meant that she recognised that, just as women and men had a common interest in struggling together against their bosses, so too did British and migrant workers.

Eleanor seems to have been the Marx who most embraced her Jewish identity. In reply to an invitation to speak at a Jewish workers' meeting in Mile End, she wrote, "I shall be very glad to speak at the meeting of 1 November [1890], the more glad that my father was a Jew." The meeting was not just about the strike, but in protest against repression and pogroms that Jewish people in the pre-revolutionary Russian Empire were suffering. Many of the Jews who lived in east London were recent migrants themselves, reflecting the long history that the area has of attracting migrant workers.

New Unionism expressed itself in the streets and squares, as well as in and around the workplaces. The May Day demonstration of 1890 was when it was at its most visible. It was here that Eleanor Marx made one of her most famous speeches. She took up the central issue of the eight-hour day as the initial subject of her speech. She argued that an Eight Hours' Bill, achieved through the strikes, should become law. She noted, "I can remember when we came in handfuls of a few dozen to Hyde Park to demand an Eight Hours' Bill, but the dozens have grown to hundreds, and the hundreds to thousands, until we have this magnificent demonstration that fills the park today" (www.marxists.org/archive/eleanor-marx/works/mayday.htm).

But she went further than just calling for reforms. She announced that "we aim at a time when there will no longer be one class supporting two others, but the unemployed both at the top and at the bottom of society will be got rid of." She ended with a quote from the poet Shelley: "Ye are many – they are few".

From Silvertown to Stepney, to the cities across Britain, New Unionism represented – without overstatement

– one of the turning points of working class history. On 7 September *The East London News'* main editorial, with the headline "Strike Fever" summed up how widespread the strikes were: "The present week might not inaptly be called the week of strikes – coal men, Match Girls, parcels postmen, carmen, rag, bone and paper porters and pickers and the employees in jam, biscuit, rope, iron, screw, clothing and railway works have found some grievance, real and imaginary and have followed the infectious example of coming out on strike" (quoted in Charlton, p99).

That "infectious example" remains an inspiration today. Workers who were told and believed for years that they could not improve their working conditions, their pay or their hours were beginning to fight back. Their example destroys the myth that anyone is "unorganisable". Eleanor played an important part in the success of New Unionism and in giving workers the confidence to fight back.

★ 12:
THE
BOSSES'
OFFENSIVE

If the 1880s was the era of strikes and protests, then the 1890s was the period when a bosses' offensive, and reformism, took hold. The spirit of New Unionism had begun to wane. The decade also marked a difficult personal period for Eleanor Marx, although she continued to be active and involved.

The bosses' offensive was sharp and vicious; workers were blacklisted and starved back to work as solidarity fell away. They had tried during the height of New Unionism to break the strikes. The scale and militancy of the action often beat them back. But in some cases, such as at Silvertown, they were successful. In the 1890s they began to win more decisively.

The police played an important role in breaking the strikes. John Tully describes how, at Silvertown, "Sam Silver [the boss] told shareholders that the 'reign of terror' of the Silvertown pickets 'might be traced to the inaction of the police' but that 'the strike collapsed when the police were firm'." He continued: "Since the dock strike, the police and government had been under intense pressure from employers and their friends in Parliament to act firmly against strikers" (Tully, p159).

In 1892, at Manningham Mill near Bradford, 3,000 workers, many of whom were women, had been on an incredibly militant strike. Their wages were being cut by a third. Their strike involved the whole community and went on for nearly six months. But with no strike pay and solidarity falling away, they were starved back to work. The bosses were resolute in their determination to stop the strike.

The new unions failed to galvanise their members and these defeats left them seriously weakened. In the first two years of the 1890s their membership fell from 320,000 to 130,000. The National Union of Gas Workers and General Labourers, in which Eleanor played such a crucial early role, had lost more than half its 60,000 members by 1896.

As the movement declined, the old unions reasserted their methods and led an attack on the approach of the new unions. George Shipton, the chair of the London Trades Council, argued that instead of using strikes and demonstrations to demand reforms from the state, the only way was to work through it. He argued: "When the people...were without votes, the only power left to them was the demonstration of numbers. Now, however, the workmen have votes" (quoted in Tony Cliff and Donny Gluckstein, *The Labour Party: A Marxist History*, Bookmarks, 1988, p9).

Of course, not all of them – the workmen or women – did have the vote. Still, over 125 years later, the arguments of Shipton and his ilk have parallels. There is a continual assertion that a Labour government will mean workers' struggles are unnecessary.

The hostility and stranglehold of the old unions meant that unity, and victory for strikes, was almost impossible. Eleanor herself felt the wrath of the established labour leaders when she was excluded from the Trades Union Congress (TUC) of 1892. She wrote, "Now, to begin with, I am a working woman – I work as a typewriter; and secondly it is surely preposterous for anyone except the Congress itself to declare who shall sit and who shall not" (quoted in Holmes, p339).

The new unions that Eleanor built and supported were much more democratic than this. Although they had committees, they also held huge meetings where every member had a say on union policy. The move by the TUC represented a bureaucratic attack on socialists and their ideas, as well as a reaffirmation of their approach.

Eleanor recognised that many of the leaders of New Unionism were being pulled towards the old bureaucracy's ways. Many became part of the established trade union bureaucracy. In 1893 Tillett blocked a national strike against mass scabbing at Hull docks. In 1894 Thorne exhorted his members to rely on the advice of their officials, declaring that "a firm stand should be made against men coming out on strike, unless oppressed to such an extent that their position is unbearable" (quotes in Cliff and Gluckstein, p10). John Burns, when he became a Liberal cabinet member, said he was tired of "working class boots, working class trains, working class houses and working class margarine" (*Socialist Worker*, "The rise and fall of New Unionism", 20 October 2009).

This was a significant shift away from the approach of Eleanor Marx, and indeed the new union leaders themselves, during the heady years of the late 1880s. Eleanor was particularly unimpressed with the pull of nationalism that was reasserting itself in the labour movement.

Socialists, although tiny in number, played a crucial

role in New Unionism and its varied successes. From organising solidarity to arguing about big political questions, socialists sought to break away from the ways of organising of the old unions and build a movement of the whole of the working class to represent their fight. They linked industrial questions with the political questions and challenged the idea that politics and economics were separate and that change came through the ballot box, maybe in alliance with the Liberal Party.

Two paths were available: representation in parliament as a substitute for the militant action seen throughout the 1880s, or a revolutionary path. And the circumstances fitted the growth of reformism. Workers, despite their defeats, were building a limited level of confidence and looked to break away from the two main parties of the time. The Liberals, many felt, no longer represented their interests. In 1893 the Independent Labour Party (ILP) was formed, led by socialist and union leader Keir Hardie. He later became Labour's first MP.

The ILP represented a new and fundamental step forward in the representation of working class people in parliament. But it was also contradictory in that it represented a move away from militant action. Instead of working class politics being played out on the streets and in the workplaces, it moved to seeking change inside the system by parliamentary methods. Because the ILP was established in a period of defeat, its politics were not up for the challenge. It was the defeats of New Unionism – not its militant and crucial successes – that gave birth to the ILP.

Eleanor continued to work internationally. She played a crucial role in establishing the Second International in

1889, which brought together socialist parties and trade unions. It wasn't just because she had friends elsewhere in the world that she recognised the importance of inter-nationalism. She argued that as capital organised across borders, so too should workers.

She continued to speak to workers and on the platforms of ILP and SDF meetings. But the spirit of New Unionism was waning. She left the executive of the union. The latter half of the 1890s marked a particularly isolating time for Eleanor. In 1895 Engels, one of her closest comrades and friends, died. She then experienced a huge personal betrayal by Edward Aveling when she discovered he had secretly married another woman.

In 1898 Eleanor Marx committed suicide by prussic acid. She had seen New Unionism, the movement that she committed so much energy and political work to, lose its spirit and its battles. But its lessons remained and so too did her impact.

★ 13:
CONCLUSION

Eleanor Marx played a big part in huge shifts in society. She would recognise the world we live in today. The period of New Unionism is one of great significance and inspiration.

Hundreds of thousands of workers showed that strikes, the more militant the better, can effect real change on their lives. The working class and its organisations had suffered a long and painful hiatus. Eleanor played a role in bringing them back to life.

Workers who were ignored by the bosses, politicians and even trade unions turned that on its head and gave birth to the modern trade union movement. New Unionism showed that things could be different.

Inspiring examples of just this sort of action continue to emerge. In 2014 fast food workers in the US, mainly black or migrant workers with little history of union organisation, fought back over poverty pay and terrible conditions. Sound familiar? One of their slogans was: "We can't survive on 7.25". The parallels with the matchwomen, dockers and gas workers are clear. So is their insistence on the right to organise "for fifteen dollars and a union!"

Closer to home too the seeds of union organisation and a real fight back have been seen among so-called "unorganisable" workers, from contract cleaners to workers in the entertainment and hospitality industry to those on zero-hours contracts.

Eleanor was a champion of the oppressed. In a society (and sometimes a workers' movement) where anti-immigrant myths were constantly perpetuated, she recognised the importance of unity between workers against their real enemies — the boss and the state. In the run-up to the 2015 elections immigration was once again a dominant theme in UK politics. In the era of austerity politicians are attacking migrants to shift the blame away from a system that doesn't deliver for ordinary people. Eleanor Marx organised for unity between migrant workers and their British counterparts. New Unionism gave the strongest and best response to such racist scapegoating.

Eleanor didn't see a separation between the interests of working class men and women, but hope in their combination. She protested against a system that subjected women to prostitution, low pay and moralistic double standards. She fought for a woman's place to be in her union. And always at the centre of her arguments was a core belief that the emancipation of the working class is the act of the working class itself.

At the end of Eleanor's life the new Labour Party was put forward as the best way to represent working class people. Political independence was a significant step forward. Demobilisation and waiting for parliamentary solutions were not.

Eleanor Marx saw an alternative: a class that organised across borders, just as the rich do. She was a champion of the oppressed who linked the everyday struggles to a big vision. Our task remains the same.

FURTHER READING

Yvonne Kapp's classic biography has long been the most authoritative account of Eleanor Marx's life and politics. Yvonne Kapp, *Eleanor Marx, vol 1: Family Life, 1855-1983*, gives an insight into Eleanor's early influences, while *Eleanor Marx, vol 2: The Crowded Years, 1884-1898* is an impressive account of her most political years. Originally published by Virago in the 1970s, both volumes are now out of print but can be tracked down second-hand or in libraries.

Rachel Holmes's biography *Eleanor Marx: A Life* (Bloomsbury, 2014) is an enjoyable introduction with emphasis on Eleanor Marx's personal, family and cultural life. It is widely available.

The best way to access Eleanor Marx's own writings and speeches is through the Marxist Internet Archive at www.marxists.org. There are also long passages quoted in Kapp's books.

John Charlton's *It Just Went Like Tinder* (Redwords, 1999) is an impressive book on New Unionism and has particularly good emphases on the Irish community and socialist organisations. It is now out of print but is available second-hand and through libraries.

Louise Raw's *Striking a Light: The Bryant and May Matchwomen and their Place in History* (Continuum, 2011) is a valuable and well-researched book on the Bryant and May matchwomen and their significance to the development of New Unionism. It also looks at the wider position of women in society and the labour movement.

Tony Cliff and Donny Gluckstein's *The Labour Party: A Marxist History* (Bookmarks, 1988) is a useful introduction to understanding the development of the early Labour Party and its links to New Unionism.

Hassan Mahamdallie's book *Crossing the 'River of Fire': the Socialism of William Morris* (Redwords, 2008) contains some excellent sections on the development of the Socialist League and the campaigns in which it was involved.

More Bookmarks Rebel's Guides

Available from Bookmarks, the socialist bookshop
1 Bloomsbury Street, London WC1B 3QE
info@bookmarksbookshop.co.uk
bookmarksbookshop.co.uk
020 7637 1848

A REBEL'S GUIDE TO MARX
Mike Gonzalez
£3
This concise and to-the-point guide offers a short, accessible introduction to the range of Marx's ideas, from his analysis of what drives corporate globalisation to his discussion of if and how human liberation can be achieved.

A REBEL'S GUIDE TO LENIN
Ian Birchall
£3
A pocket guide to the real Lenin, showing the complexities behind a man often vilified by historians. It shows his methods and motivations in attempting to create a world in which production was to be for human need rather than profit.

SEXISM AND THE SYSTEM:
A REBEL'S GUIDE TO WOMEN'S LIBERATION
Judith Orr
£3
We are told that women are now equal
to men and there's nothing left to fight
for. This is the socialist case for women's
liberation which argues why winning this
battle means changing the world.

A REBEL'S GUIDE TO TROTSKY
Esme Choonara
£3
Many people have heard the name, Leon
Trotsky – but how many know anything
about his life or his ideas? Trotsky was
a central figure in the decisive event of
the 20th century, the Russian Revolution
of 1917.

A REBEL'S GUIDE TO ROSA LUXEMBURG
Sally Campbell
£3
Rosa Luxemburg was one of the key
leaders of the German revolutionary left
until her murder by right wing militiamen
in 1919 at the height of the attempted
revolution. She was an orator, teacher
and leader.